The urgent needs that come with managing a busy household pull at you for your attention, holding you back from doing the things that you know your family needs most. You feel caught in a tug-a-war between the urgent and best. Something needs to change. How do you get your family from where it is to where you know it should be? Let's find out together!

Contents

Preface

My fellow weary mama, how many times do we find ourselves overwhelmed and at our wits' end, feeling pulled in too many directions at once? Our obligations are endless as we're expected to be wearing multiple hats at any given moment- cook, secretary, chauffeur, nurse, referee, maid, teacher, accountant, interior decorator, fashion coordinator, counselor... SO many hats! How are we to keep from being constantly frazzled and depleted? I've identified only FOUR main hats that moms should wear. Moms need to focus on wearing the hats of MASTER GARDENER, MANAGER of the MONKEYS (I *don't* mean your kids), VISIONARY, and BAROMETER. We're going to look at these four areas of responsibility, get a new perspective on all the crazy obligations, and implement some practical solutions for reducing the chaos. All of this with a goal of enjoying and celebrating Your Family, God's Masterpiece!

The Harrison Family 2018

And so, I'd like you to meet my family, God's masterpiece. The Great Creator imagined us, designed us, and is still molding us each day. Not one of these individuals is perfect but each of us is an essential element of His "Harrison Artwork." The scars we each have are also beautiful parts of each one of us as they represent God's loving hand of healing and transformation. The ways He has crafted our strengths, and the way He shapes improvements in our weaknesses are a tribute to His craftsmanship. He has specific works that He wants each of us to accomplish as ambassadors of His love and mercy. We are His artwork, existing for His glory.

Ephesians 2:10 "For we are God's workmanship, created in Christ Jesus, to do good works that He prepared in advance for us to do."

Are you ready to launch into the philosophy behind the four main hats that a mom should wear to remain laser-focused in this most worthy journey – being the masterpiece family that God designed you to be? Come on, let's do this together!

Chapter 1: It's a Trap!

Literally 50 at any given moment – that's about how many hats we moms try to wear every day, ALL DAY. We wear all these hats and then jump on the proverbial hamster wheel of daily life. The hats don't fit in the wheel and every time we start running some of the hats fall off. We climb down to get the hats and then jump back on again only to knock off more hats. No matter how hard we try, we don't seem to make any headway and we feel like we're constantly failing.

So, is this really the way God intended the mom-life to look?

Your Family Has a Target on Its Back

One troublesome reason why the mom-life is so hard is because our family has been targeted by a great enemy. Did you know that there's a target on your family's back? There's one on my family as well. The Bible tells us in John 10:10a that we have an enemy (Satan) who comes to "steal, kill, and destroy." He wants to steal every mother's self-worth, our physical health, our sanity and our joy. He wants to kill our marriages and destroy our families. His main mode of operation is to LIE and DISTRACT. Remember when Jesus was fasting in the desert and Satan tempted Jesus with a false reality: Satan promised to give Jesus all the kingdoms of the world if only he would bow at Satan's feet. (Satan didn't actually have the power to give those kingdoms to anyone and Jesus had authority over Satan. Thus, there was no merit to Satan's offer). That's what Satan does - he lies, he distorts or perverts that which was created for good, and he tempts with false images.

Moms are susceptible to this liar's mirage as well. You know what false view Satan loves to show to us moms? He likes to take us to the false image of Super Mom raising Super Kid living in Super House. The lie is that if we really care about our kids we'll give them everything, we'll turn them into the best at everything, and we'll look and act like a Super Model while we achieve this ultimate, thrilling life! This view is a fake, my mom friend. It can't be attained.

He fashions it to make us feel like failures, to distract us from the things that really matter and, worst of all, to sneak in and infiltrate our camp when we are weary and defeated. He tricks us into picking up all those hats and getting on that dead-end wheel. Moms, it's a trap! Don't fall for it!

In contrast to the one who wants to steal, kill, and destroy, Scripture tells us that Christ came so that we can experience "an abundant life" (John 10:10b). I think we could all agree that frazzled chaos and constant obligations are not exactly abundant living. As Christ followers and as moms who love our kids immensely, I'll bet that your true desire for your kids is that they would become adults who are living in the middle of God's specifically fashioned will for their individual lives. Being the greatest ever 7th-grade all-star athlete or graduating with a 4.0 GPA pales in comparison to living out God's intended purpose for your son or daughter, with his or her unique talents and passions, wouldn't you agree? And yet we find ourselves daily running hard on our little hamster wheel, feeling frantic and weak-kneed as we continually aim for the false image. If this crazy hamster-wheel, fifty-hat life isn't what Christ intended for us, how in the world can we get to that truly abundant life that He *did* intend? Well, I have a few suggestions for you to learn how to wear all your hats without wearing out and it actually begins by realizing that *you may be wearing the wrong hats altogether.*

Truth: <u>While you may FEEL like your mom job description is to do everything, Your Role is NOT to do Everything!</u>

If you try to do everything, four negative things happen:

1. **You DON'T accomplish what GOD has intended for you to accomplish because you're busy doing other things.**

2. **OTHERS DON'T accomplish what God intended for THEM to accomplish because you're doing their things.** *(Do you hear that, mom? You might be doing things that God intended for your kids to do or your friend or your sister or your husband, and you're robbing them of the blessings associated with those accomplishments.)*

3. **Trying to do everything keeps you at your WORST**. *(You know how it is when you've said "yes" to help with way too many activities and you end up doing a poor job at all of them because you really can only do so much. Trying to do everything means we end up doing a lot of things poorly.)*

4. **Trying to do everything for your family makes your family and the individuals in the family WEAK.** *(If we consistently do a task for someone when that someone is capable of doing that task for himself, we just make him weaker in that area and more dependent on us. We want our kids to thrive as adults,*

9

not be dependent on mom forever. When your kids serve others, work hard, and even go without some desires, it makes them stronger.)

Ephesians 2:10 says,
"You are God's artwork created in Christ Jesus to do good works which He PREPARED in advance for YOU to do."

God says your life is artwork that includes specific good works that He prepared for you to do and that your kids are artwork that includes specific good works that He prepared for each of them to do. (By the way, all that artwork that God made in your family, the combination of that artwork is a marvelous one-of-a-kind masterpiece!) As for the work that is left after that, there could be someone else in your life who is intended to do some of those tasks - a grandparent, an aunt, an older lonely neighbor, etc. *(My mother is a skilled singer and she loves giving my kids voice lessons while my dad is a great geography and history resource for us. I used to hire a single church friend to come one afternoon per week to do a bunch of bulk cooking for me.*

She would make some breakfast burritos, baked goods and main entree dishes in three hours a week. This freed me up to focus on the kids and it didn't cost any more to me than one meal out for our family would have cost. The kids always looked forward to her coming and I believe she enjoyed the time with them as well - I generally would pick two kids a week to be her helper.) What about the rest of the things that need to get done? (WARNING, shocking statement to follow): It is right for some things to not get done. No really, if the kids have to eat a pb&j, a handful of lettuce and an apple for dinner because your shopping isn't scheduled until tomorrow, that's okay. That might not be a conventional dinner meal, but it'll help them to appreciate when you do cook a great meal.

You've been spending all this time trying to wear 50 hats and trying to catch them as they quickly fall off. Girl, you aren't supposed to be wearing all those hats! Stop trying to do   EVERYTHING!

I've been a mom for twenty-four years to seven treasured children and, sadly, I've worn the wrong hats far too many times, which has meant plenty of regrets. Through lots of prayer, reading the Bible (the best parent guidebook ever!) as well as lots of other parenting books and learning from my mistakes, I've identified four basic "mom-hats" that give us a more abundant life. Those four hats are Master Gardener, Manager of the Monkeys (not our kids), Visionary, and Barometer. Hopefully, this information will bring some clarity, relief, and peace to your overworked soul.

Chapter 2:

Master Gardener Hat

Do you ever feel like you are struggling constantly but never making any progress in your role as a mom? You know motherhood is valuable, but you feel so overwhelmed by all the "hats" you're supposed to wear, such as cook, chauffeur, and counselor, just to name a few. Moms feel pressure to wear all these hats while modeling the latest SUPER MOM attire, toting around little SUPER KID who *must be* best at everything he participates in, and he participates in pretty much EVERYTHING because, after all, he is SUPER KID! How do we stop the insanity?! In chapter one of "Wearing All Your Hats Without Wearing Out" I told you about our enemy, Satan (a liar and deceiver), who aims to destroy our families. Just like he tempted Jesus in the desert, the Devil loves to tell a mom that she must be SUPER MOM or else she will be FAILURE MOM. So, moms do their very best to wear all of these hats that seem IMPOSSIBLE to wear and wind up feeling defeated by all the pressure.

If we mothers are not supposed to do everything, how do we figure out what we are supposed to do?

I have identified four main hats that a mom should wear: **Master Gardener, Manager of the Monkeys** (and I don't mean your kids), **Visionary, and Barometer.**

The truth that our enemy doesn't want us to think about is that we as moms are not supposed to be chasing the supposedly *ideal* Super Mom image. A main hat that God wants moms to wear is the hat of Master Gardener, for, instead of running on a hamster wheel, we are to be tending a garden. This garden is growing the most priceless of plants - our children. Gardeners know that much hard work is necessary before we see results, but the gardener does all of this because of her love for the plants and the anticipation of the beautiful springtime blossoms to come. When I think of my children's futures, what does their "life in bloom" look like? For me, I see it as a time when all their abilities, experiences, and passions come

together to display God's glory through them as they pursue God's specifically fashioned will for their individual life. That image will take many years to come to fruition. That's their life in bloom and that's why I tend the garden, working to help them have strong souls, minds, and bodies that are *someday* going to be a fascinating masterpiece, a collage of God's intricate involvement in their lives. It is not going to necessarily look great *today* - the soil is dirty, the sun is hot, there are some weeds to take out, some pests to purge, and even some pruning to do before the beautiful blooms come.

Your child's life will grow and bloom and blossom in time.

How's your patience? Because if you want the best kinds of blooms - the ones that really last, with large beautiful petals, it's going to require patience and consistency. When my seven kiddos were all little and I was so tired and overwhelmed, I would muster up the energy to train them AGAIN on how to handle the current squabble or dispute between them, or I'd reluctantly give consequences for not following through with a task AGAIN. I would wonder if taking this time on their character was really worth it. Now that most of them are grown, I see their lives and characters flourishing and it makes me so thankful that we made their **character development a top priority.**

All plants have some basic needs that should be consistently met - providing sunlight, water, and soil while giving protection from weather and harmful pests. If we overdue any of the essentials, our treasured plants start to die: too much sunlight, they wither; too much water, they rot; too deep in the soil and they can't sprout. In general, moms these days feel an obligation to *overdo everything* with our kids rather than giving them *enough*. As a gardener, we need to give our plants *enough*, not too little and not too much. Satan wants us to believe that we should give our kids too much - do everything for them, give them

everything, make them the very best at everything (there's a difference between doing things with excellence in a balanced life and winning all categories at the cost of our family's sanity and peace). Until the plants (our children) are strong enough to withstand the environment on their own, we need to provide protection from inclement weather while also eliminating choking weeds and unwanted pests. Mother gardeners are protecting our children from destructive elements until their roots are deep and their trunks are stout enough to withstand the harmful elements of the world.

As we grow our gardens, moms don't want to be just any old gardener. We want to be Master Gardeners (and by *"Master"* I mean that we look to the Master, our Lord Jesus) to see how best to raise these priceless plants under our care. We read about how the Master told us to handle life in His word, we listen for the voice of the Master who is giving us specific direction for our day, and we implement changes in our lives to align with Him).

Jesus, our example for living abundantly in all areas, is even an example to us in the reality that not all things are to get done: The crowds were following Jesus, wanting Him to heal them and teach them. Pretty soon He chose to get in a boat to get some distance from the crowd and He even *took a nap*! (Mark 4:38) Sure, he cared about the crowds and He wanted to meet the people's needs, but He also knew *there was only so much that He was intended to do at that moment*. Another time, when his mother asked Him to change the water into wine at the wedding feast, he did do what she asked but He also told her that it wasn't the right time for Him to be doing miracles yet (John 2:4). Similarly, he scolded the disciples when they fussed at the woman who poured expensive perfume on His feet when He said, "the poor you will always have with you, but you will only have me for a little while" (John 12:3).

In other words, Jesus was saying, *"Disciples, there will always be poor people that she can help, but this is the only moment in which she can spend this*

time with me. Do not overlook this precious moment in which I want her to focus on me." This is an example of what I call a "God-moment" and I believe that **one of the most important ways to be a Master Gardener mom is to be always on the lookout for the potential "God Moments" in our children's days**. Jesus could say something similar to mothers by saying, *"There will always be floors to vacuum, dishes to*

wash, kids that need to get somewhere on time and meals to figure out, but wait... do you see this more valuable, fleeting God-moment in your child's life right now? Do not be distracted by the things of this world." Jesus was showing that it is best to **Slow down and experience this most vital and irreplaceable experience that He has prepared for your family.** Stop and linger there in those God-moments, even enjoy them. Take the time to abundantly live the God-moments of your children's

days. Train your children to listen for His quiet and gentle voice, to watch for Him at work in your family's needs and in your blessings, help your kids to identify His fingerprints on the world around them. Soak up those moments and let God saturate these times with your family. Lead by example in being a sheep who listens for His voice and who lingers in the green pastures of His presence.

Moms, the false view of "Super-Mom and Super-Star Kid" carries an empty promise that leads to all the wrong things, such as emotional and physical burnout. The amazing thing about God and His ways is that when we focus on the right things- like the God-moments in each day, He brings to fruition many of those other hopes and desires of our hearts, but He does it in His way, in His timing, and in ways that bring Him glory. A Master Gardener (in this case, a gardener who follows *the Master)* isn't focused on the scurry and hurry of the rest of the world, rather she is

OUR DAUGHTER BECCA AND OUR FIRST GRANDSON

focused on patiently, consistently tending her garden and **this Master Gardener is especially focused on the God-moments that are the best nourishment of all for her growing plants.**

How can we identify the God-moments when all day is chaos? Oh, now here is the key! You must organize and delegate - **for you cannot identify the God-moments in the midst of chaos and disorganization**. And, so, we come to the next appropriate mom hat, **Manager of the Monkeys**.

Chapter 3:

Manager of the
Monkeys
(and I don't mean
your kids!)

"Well," you are saying to me, "now isn't that a warm-fuzzy image about God-moments and gardens, but for the real world I have bills that need to be paid, kids who are hungry for lunch, and quite frankly I'd like a shower today."

Mom, I get it; I hear you. What I've figured out in my own life is that it's a wrong paradigm to think that I should be the sole cook, maid, seamstress, and every other task that is needed to have a family, but I am the Manager of all those needs. *There's a difference psychologically and physically in a paradigm of "all the tasks are mom's hats to wear" versus "mom manages the tasks and who they belong to," which means doing some, delegating some, dumping some, and letting some go undone.*

Let's look specifically at the tasks that you need to be delegating to your children, often referred to as "chores." Are you sure you're delegating chores EFFECTIVELY?

Let's say you walk into the bathroom and see that your four-year-old son brushed his teeth and left toothpaste-spit in the sink. Lovely. Before you go off to scold him or give him consequences, you should ask yourself, "Okay, I taught him how to BRUSH his teeth, but have I ever clearly shown him how to clean up after he's done brushing?" If the answer is, "no," then frankly, you can only blame yourself for that lovely little mess in the sink. Training a child in what excellence looks like in a given task requires some time but it is well worth it!

Keep reading, I'd like to show you how DELEGATING TASKS can be best for the entire family, including your kids!

Delegating jobs to our kids is not a cop-out on *our* responsibilities. Rather it is teaching them to be responsible, which prepares them for abundant living as adults while it also gives them a sense of accomplishment and self-sufficiency now. I wanted my kids to have a visual of me giving them a "responsibility" so I use the phrase "monkey on your back" to describe giving them a task that I want them to own. I'll often tell my kids, "I am giving this 'monkey' to you. Own your monkey."

Recently my youngest son, a junior in high school, asked me what his password login is for the ACT prep account that I had just set up for him. While I didn't mind looking up the password and giving it to him, I didn't want to look it up multiple times- when he asks again tomorrow and the day after, etc. I could instead make him in charge of something that should be appropriately his. But it **wouldn't** be **effectively** giving him that "monkey" if I said, "now don't forget this password because I don't want to tell you again." Instead, **I want to equip him with a success habit that will help him throughout life.** So, I told him, "get a little notebook and label it, "Andrew's Passwords.' " Then when I told him what his password was, it was the only time I would need to give it to him because I was passing the 'password monkey' to him which was both saving me time in the long run and giving him a system for being self-sufficient in this area.

As a mom, I wear the hat of MANAGER of the MONKEYS: identifying what to **Do, Delegate, Dump and leave UN-Done**. For those tasks that need to be delegated to my children, I make these decisions  <u>prayerfully</u> because I really do believe that God wants to be developing different character qualities at different times in each of my kids. <u>I try to delegate jobs by assigning them to the YOUNGEST one *capable* of doing each task.</u> Notice that I said, "capable" not "knowledgeable about" that task. *If I am constantly evaluating what my kids are capable of doing, then I am constantly increasing their ability and self-sufficiency.* **Resist the temptation to give the monkey to the one who you can most easily hand it off to,** such as the oldest or the one who won't complain about it, **because this Manager of the Monkeys role is not about making life easier for you, it is about GROWING your kids' abilities, character, work ethic, attitude...** Honestly, usually the one who complains the most about a task, is the one who needs to be assigned that task because they've clearly got more character development needed in that area.

(Emma, 6, excited to learn to clean windows. Don't worry, we no longer use chemicals for this chore - Hydrogen peroxide works so much better!

At our house, the quickest way to be given more work is to have a complaining or sluggish attitude in completing a chore. When we allow complaining, we actually are keeping them focused on the negative in situations and allowing them to have no emotional self-control. Once this bad habit is reduced, you can imagine how more peaceful and pleasant a home can be! (By complaining, I'm referring to an attitude of whininess).

I'm not suggesting that we shouldn't hear our kids out when they want to talk about some suggestions on how to do chores more effectively in some way or brainstorming on how to make it more fun, even. I want them to think and reason and create, I just don't want them to habitually complain. I'll reward ingenuity all day long, but I'm not **rewarding** complaining ever.

ABBY AND EMMA COOKING TOGETHER

A home where work is usually done pleasantly with best effort results in your having way more time for fun and freedom as you haven't wasted time on kids complaining about the job and trying to weasel out of the job, mom nagging about the job or having to have a child redo the job because the quality of work was poor. Just think of how much time is freed up when we get those issues taken care of! **Consider your children's future employers and spouses, and the success that they'll experience in those situations because they learned to own their task, with excellence as their standard, and all with a joyful attitude. Now that's an atmosphere of abundant living for each person in the family!**

(Don't send me comments about my being unreasonable and raising robot kids. The truth is that whining, complaining, and low-quality standards equals a much UNHAPPIER life for your kids and is definitely not something I want for my kids. I can confidently say this because I have tried the other way – several times. Each time I would start to think maybe I'm being unreasonable to expect a good attitude while working, my grumpy child would just get grumpier and grumpier. Then when I'd go back to expecting a good attitude from them, it seemed to consistently produce contentment in them. It's no different for any of us adults, either- when we decide it's okay to be grumpy, we become grumpier. When we determine that life is better when we are content, we become more content and suddenly our circumstances don't seem as dire either. The Bible tells us to take every thought captive. Developing the habit of determining to be positive only brightens our future.)

A life of abundance is only possible if we reduce bad habits that keep us from joy, peace, and freedom. *While we're on this topic, I will also say, if they have learned emotional and physical self-control, developing good habits in these areas, then when they have an off day where they're not displaying these qualities, you as mom are able to quickly identify that something is going on with that child and you want to figure out what's up. I refer to this as being the "Barometer" in your child's life, and that's the third* *mom-hat. You can learn more about being a Barometer of your kids in chapter five.*

So, just to sum this up- we moms are encouraged to believe that all the various tasks in our lives are **an obligatory mom-hat and our worth as a mom is based on how well we complete all those tasks. But those tasks are, actually, just tasks. They're not the main thing about motherhood. In fact, many of those tasks, if dispersed appropriately, are just right for developing your kids into people who experience Abundant Living!**

How to Hand Off a Monkey: Effectively DELEGATING

Show it. Watch it. Praise it. Repeat.

Then follow-up with

*Standard of Excellence

*Appropriate Consequences

*Praising what you want Repeated

When you give a task to one of your children for the first time it requires DETAILED TRAINING: Show It, Watch It, Praise it, Repeat, Follow-up. *Show them what doing this task with excellence as the standard* looks like by *you doing it while they watch, then having them do it while you*

watch, being coach and cheerleader while you're watching, correcting with a standard of excellence, praising a job well done. Yes, this process does require a big chunk of time the first time you delegate a particular "monkey" to a particular child (and perhaps even needs to be repeated the second time you assign this task to that child, depending on the child's age and the complexity of the task), but in the long run, thorough training as you delegate something new SAVES a great deal of time and results in a much more smoothly functioning home.

Remember, one of our goals in delegating is to eliminate the chaos that is keeping us from identifying the God-moments in our days.

It is worth it! So effective delegation steps are: Show it. Watch it. Praise it. Repeat, and one more step, Follow-up – to see how their task ended up.

Recently my youngest child, age eight, had been tasked with cleaning and cutting the radishes. When I came and checked the job afterwards I saw that she

31

had left the stems and leaves on the counter and hadn't put away the container of radishes either. **I could have cleaned up her mess myself and that would have been quicker in the moment, but it wouldn't have produced the character in her that we're aiming for and it would mean she would continue to work with a low standard in the future.**

I went and found her in another room and led her back to the kitchen to take a look at the mess. I asked, "What is incomplete about this job?" She immediately knew that she hadn't really finished because I've told her many times, **"A job isn't complete unless it's cleaned up and put away."** *She said,* **"I didn't finish cleaning up and putting it away,"** *so I had her finish the job and gave her an extra job because I need her to know that* **"incomplete work always has some consequences".** *I didn't give her an extra job AND a scolding, just an extra job. I used to do both (and still fall into that trap on occasion), but I have learned that gently spoken consequences are much more effective than lecturing and much less harmful to our relationship.*

Following up after a task may be time-consuming, at the moment, but it will create a much more peaceful, less chaotic home in the long run as well as producing character qualities that are necessary for abundant living. Hebrews 12:11 says, "No discipline seems pleasant at the time, but painful. Later on, however, it produces a harvest of righteousness and peace for those who have been trained by it." **If you delegate with quality training, appropriate expectations, and consistent follow-up**

32

with necessary consequences as needed, it will pay off both in relieving of workload for you AND (most importantly) it will be wonderful character development for your children's abundant life!

Hebrews 12:11 says, "No discipline seems pleasant at the time, but painful. Later on, however, it produces a harvest of righteousness and peace for those who have been trained by it."

Chapter 4:

Visionary Hat

My fellow weary mothers, how many times do we find ourselves overwhelmed and at our wits' end, feeling pulled in too many directions at once? Our obligations are endless as we're expected to be wearing multiple hats at any given moment- cook, secretary, chauffeur, nurse, referee, maid, teacher, counselor...

SO many hats! How are we to keep from being constantly frazzled and depleted? I've identified only FOUR main hats that moms should wear. Moms need to focus on wearing the hats of MASTER GARDENER, MANAGER of the MONKEYS (I *don't* mean your kids), VISIONARY, and BAROMETER.

Have you seen the newest non-animated version of Cinderella (Disney 2015)? Near the beginning of the story we see Cinderella receive a small but powerful message at the deathbed of her birth mother. Five simple words, "Have courage and be kind," guided Cinderella throughout her difficult early years when she had plenty of opportunity to be resentful, vindictive, and angry. At the end of the movie, when she has married the prince, we watch her humbly and mercifully forgive her step-mother. Cinderella's mother had spoken life into Cinderella's soul, blessing her with love by visualizing Cinderella's character as kind and brave. She could see it in her mother's eyes and hear it in her voice that her mother truly *believed* that Cinderella would be brave and kind, that she had the ability to be that caliber of person no matter what would come her way, and it is that visionary blessing that carried the young girl through all of her many hardships.

Scripture says that we hold the power of LIFE and DEATH in our TONGUE (Proverbs 18:21). The words we as parents choose to make all the difference in whether or not we are CASTING a VISION of abundant life - the look in our eye and the sound of our voice as we're saying we believe our child was created for good things (motivating her to excellence in efforts, kindness in interactions, and bravery in the adventures of life which all lead to abundant living). Or we hold the power of death in our words - diminishing the child's worth, demotivating them from striving for seemingly unattainable excellence, demanding a good behavior on the outside while not shaping their heart for good on the inside. (Matthew 23:27). I am sad to say that I have learned many hard lessons about the power of word choice, tone, and the look in my eye when speaking to my kids and I will always regret these mistakes. This is the area in which I have failed the most as a mom and God has helped me to overcome so many incorrect perspectives about this area of parenthood.

Because my natural personality type is Dominant - someone who tends to think that they're always right and their way is always the best way - you can imagine how difficult I have made life for my kids from time to time, especially before I started to recognize the great importance of our words and attitudes, and our vision for our kids. My strongest-willed son was also my firstborn son. Sadly, I had not learned the importance of being a visionary with my words when he was younger. I would scold him with words like, "Why do you always do that?" or "Stop *always* horsing around," etc. <u>My tone</u> and the <u>look on my face</u> only further repeated the harsh statements. I was telling him that he *was* those negative behaviors. Compounding that was that the other kids would hear me say those things. How terrible! I didn't realize it at the time, but it hurt his self-worth even more that his siblings heard those negative words spoken over him and it would affect their words of him as well. **Sarcasm, condescending answers, or negative jokes are all examples of the negative power of a parent's tongue** and all are things that I've had to work on personally. While I have done everything I know to do to rectify and repair the damage that I caused him and our relationship, this remains one of the biggest regrets of my life! I am convinced that regret is one of the most miserable feelings in all of humanity because there is no hope for a re-do in regret. Some things in life, (*actually, for most things* *in life*) we don't get do-overs. I heard a wonderful quote that has helped me a lot in managing my regret, which said, "While it is good to look at the past to learn from it, don't ever feed the past. Feed the future." I will always have to live with this regret, but I am determined to put my efforts into having an abundant relationship with my son and to give him *now* the blessing and vision that he deserved all along. **Thankfully, God is a God of transformation, making beauty from ashes (Isaiah 61:1-3).** Multiple times in my journey of motherhood, I've experienced the gift of forgiveness from my kids, and seen God remake the brokenness that I had caused.

"He will give a crown of beauty for ashes, a joyous blessing instead of mourning…"

Isaiah 61:3

Here's another example of being a VISIONARY to our kids: It's Wednesday morning and Eight-year-old Emma's laundry day. She brings down her laundry and I stand with her in the laundry room while she sorts items into categories as we talk about laundry do's and don'ts. I notice that she had put a dress into her dirty clothes that wasn't actually dirty. Would you believe this is a positive opportunity?! This is a

great chance to help her develop her character and learn more about God's design for her life -even to let her know that God fashioned her with his careful, intentional design because she is so highly valued by Him, and that her actions should match that intentional care.

After asking her some questions, we figured out together that she did what was *"EASY"* instead of what was "BEST." I want to convey with my <u>words, facial expression,</u> and<u> the look in my eye</u> that I believe she was meticulously crafted by God with all the treasured details that make up our dear Emma and, likewise, her work and creations and actions should be a reflection of that

same caliber. Because I'm mom and wear the hat of VISIONARY, I want to give her a vision of herself as one who lives by the standard **"I do what is BEST, not what is EASY."** I can give her some examples in scripture of how God blessed the person who did the BEST thing instead of the EASY thing. I can point out sometimes that I remember when she or someone we know did the BEST thing even though it was hard. And we can pray and ask God to help both of us be strong enough to choose the BEST over the EASY.

To do all of this with my daughter takes a lot of extra time right now, but it has long term great benefits for her life development and it wasn't as destructive to our relationship as scolding her would have been. If this is a topic that I have taught to her previously (especially recently) then I would need to choose a consequence instead of a talk (some reasonable consequences might be to do an extra load of laundry or teach her how to iron her dress that is now wrinkled or have her clean out her closet to donate some items toward a charity to help her remember that there are poor children who wish they had a dress like hers). While I may need to give a consequence for her choice in this situation because I want her to know that **choices have consequences**, when I deliver the consequence I try to do it with an attitude of, *"I am so sad to have to give this consequence but it's important because you are a person who makes good decisions, and this wasn't a good decision. Our goal is that this consequence will help you to remember to make decisions based on what is BEST, not what is EASY." As a parent, avoid an attitude of "I have no compassion for your situation since you brought it on yourself."*

Mom, learn from MY mistake that a **sarcastic tone from the parent hurts relationship and diminishes the character development opportunity for the child**. *Show compassion in your consequence. For example, you could say, "I remember when I was a kid and instead of sweeping the floor the way I knew I was supposed to, I swept all the dirt under the rug. I got in big trouble with my mom for doing that. It's no fun to be in trouble."*

We look to the Heavenly Father as a VISIONARY to all of us- He tells us who we were made to be (Jeremiah 1:5), tells us He adores us (Jeremiah 31:3, Psalm 17:8), tells us we were not made for weakness and sin (Romans 6:2). God is the Great BLESSING Giver, our Vision-Caster for a life abundant! Just as God tells us that He LOVES US UNCONDITIONALLY beyond measure, we need to find meaningful ways to do this with our children.

The second part of being our child's visionary is by clearly letting them know WHO WE EXPECT THEM TO BE. For example, my strongest-willed daughter could have been generally labeled "little miss pride pants"- while the youngest, telling everyone else what to do and how to do it "right" as often as she could. (You think maybe she inherited her

41

mama's dominant personality?) I would have to tell her regularly, "You are a kind and humble girl, so you don't sound bossy to your siblings. You're not their boss or policeman, you're their cheerleader. As their cheerleader you say, *'Wow, good try, Abby! 'Thanks for your help, Josh'.*" I was giving her a vision of who she is meant to be and spoke that positive label over her. By age eight she had drastically improved in being kind and humble-hearted with others. (Y*es, there was also consequences along the way to help get her attention on the importance of these matters*). She's not perfect, but greatly improved.

We have to be careful with our words, careful to be sure to speak vision of abundant life and not a vision of sin and failure to them. And it shouldn't just be our words only, but also our tone and the look on our face should also say, "I see this vision for you, my child."

(For more insight on this topic, read the books THE BLESSING authored by Gary Smalley and John Trent (Smalley, 1986), as well as The Way of the Wild Heart (Eldridge, 2006).

Chapter 5:

Barometer Hat

Barometers measure atmospheric pressure. As weather forecasters monitor air pressure, observing these measurements can signal warnings that bad weather is coming or is already there. Just like a Barometer gauges the pressure in the air, moms need to be the barometers of the atmosphere of our children, observing how they are doing emotionally, spiritually, physically, and socially. When we see signs of high or low pressure, we need to find out what's going on. Don't be quick to make assumptions, but rather ask lots of questions. You might need to get them out of the normal routine to get them talking, maybe go for a drive, put a puzzle together or take them for ice cream.

Find a happy setting to find out what's going on. When I was a teenager, the only way my mom could get me to share from my heart was to go for walks together. There was something about not having to look at each other that helped me to open-up to her.

We need to remain vigilant on monitoring the pressure in our kids' lives. (Uncomfortable alert) AND we need to be monitoring if WE are the cause of some of the troubles. Our personality type plays a big role in what kind of parent we are. For instance, a dominant personality, like myself, leans more to being focused on RULES and being weak on RELATIONSHIPS while a more gentle-spirited or fun-loving parent type might lean toward RELATIONSHIP and tend to be weak on RULES. **We have to balance both BOUNDARIES (Rules) and BOUNDLESS LOVE with our child, consistently LOVING and consistently JUST.** Well known author and expert on parenting teenagers, Josh McDowell says, ***"Rules without Relationship leads to Rebellion."*** I agree, but I also believe that **Mercy Only without Boundaries and Consequences ALSO leads to Rebellion**. It takes consistency from both to maintain a healthy relationship and a healthy relationship with our child is key to being able to be

We have to balance both boundaries and boundless love for our child, consistently LOVING and consistently JUST.

44

an effective Barometer in their lives. The Barometer Hat is essential for moms because it truly is a hat best worn by a mother. We know what "normal" on their gauge looks like, we know what extenuating factors may be going into the high or low barometric pressure (perhaps they're worried about Grandpa who just had a heart attack so they couldn't sleep last night, or they are having a hard time adjusting to their sister who has gotten married and no longer has as much time for the younger sibling) and these extenuating circumstances are causing some real grumpiness symptoms. You as mom care more about all of the stuff that is going on in their lives than anyone else and thus you're in the best position to evaluate the attitudes and actions and words that are coming from your child.

Wearing the Barometer Hat well means:

1. Be Observant.

Are they spending an usual amount of time in their room or sleeping extra? Has their personality suddenly become very closed and withdrawn? Has their attitude become very negative? Are they acting out in uncharacteristic ways? These are all signs that the barometric pressure has risen and you want to find out what's causing it. Unusually bad behavior *(behavior that is not usual FOR THAT CHILD)* is not typically a time for consequences, it's a cry for help. You want to be watching to see how they are doing **a) Spiritually, b) Emotionally, c) Physically, d) Socially, e) Academically** *while you work to get to the bottom of what's causing the symptoms. Of course, sometimes consequences may be necessary, but **if it is not normal behavior for the child, see it as more of a sign to YOU, their barometer, that there is a problem you need to identify, rather than just jumping into a "quick fix" of behavior modification**. Consequences are best suited for repeated bad habits or repeated bad actions or passivity, not unusual behavior.*

2. Keep the Relationship in good standing. *It will take much effort to protect the parent/child relationship during the "storms" that blow into your child's life, but it is so important to maintain that relationship if you want to adequately wear the hat of Barometer. If you are a parent who tends to be DOMINANTING and CONTROLLING by nature, work on Filling your child's LOVE TANK, letting them know you **unconditionally adore** them If you are a parent who tends to be extra MERCIFUL and EASY GOING, work on developing **consistency in following through with appropriate consequences**. Parents who are too merciful (showing*

mercy when they should be displaying boundaries) will often end up with rebellious kids because those children interpret this as insecurity in the parent. Thus, the teenager, believing the parent isn't respecting his or her own parental authority, is not respectful of the parents' authority either. My father had strict rules and expected excellence in everything we did, but he also consistently displayed a joyful, adoring, selfless love for us that made me honor him. Even though I didn't like how strict his rules were, I honored his rules because I respected him. **Keeping the parent/child relationship in good standing is a delicate balance of both Consistent Unwavering Standard delivered by Merciful Relationship.**

3. Seek More Information. As your child's *Barometer when you recognize a change in pressure, it's time to investigate, not to "come down hard on them." Ask lots of questions but be careful to not make the child feel like he is on the witness stand and you're judging his answers, seeking to catch him being inaccurate or using his words against him to get him in trouble.* **There is a place for parents to judge their**

There is a time for parents to critique their children's words, but when we want them to open up, we need them to know that we are trustworthy with their vulnerability.

children's words, but when we want them to open up, we need them to know that we are trustworthy with their vulnerability.

Instead, you want to listen without judgement at this point or he is sure to clam- up again. Be a **SAFE HAVEN** for him to talk to you. *Just listen and pray that God will give you the right words to keep him talking. Sometimes just the process of talking it out can help your child to move past the pressure. If not, you can brainstorm together on solutions. Be sure to* **give your child the opportunity to identify some solutions for themselves and be sure to cast the vision that you believe in their ability to handle this situation with integrity and wisdom.** *Sometimes just knowing you, the parent, believes in him is all he needs to muster up the courage to tackle the problem.) Refer to "Mercy Seat Parenting" later in this book for more on parenting in a way that keeps kids open to sharing their heart with you, even on difficult issues.*

In review, rather than feeling like we should wear 50 hats at once, Moms need to focus on the four hats that only parents can wear in our child's life:

MASTER GARDENER

MANAGER OF THE MONKEYS

VISIONARY

and **BAROMETER**

There is one thing that should be a part of every one of the hats you wear, mom. That one thing is

PRAYER. Our Heavenly Father loves your kids even more than you do, and He knows them better than you do, as He made them. He is the source for all the solutions your family needs and you can trust His leading. Isaiah 40:11 says that "He gently leads those who have young." In everything you do, dear mother, breath prayer throughout every word spoken, breath in prayer through every deep breath of concern or fear or worry or contemplation. Turn all of those concerns over to God because YOU ARE NOT RESPONSIBLE FOR THE OUTCOME of your children's lives. **There is no perfect formula that will always produce perfect children. Ultimately God has given every person free will and once your children are adults, the outcome of their lives are based on their choices (among other things) but what You are RESPONSIBLE for is how you tend the garden of their growth, how you give them the tools to be self-sufficient with excellence, what kinds of vision you cast for their futures, and your efforts at gauging how they are doing emotionally, spiritually, physically, and socially as they grow.**

Remember that God isn't watching your performance with a magnifying glass to catch all your minute errors along the way. No, He is filling in the gaps in your errors (for we all have plenty of those, as we are human). Isaiah 40:11 "He tends His flock like a shepherd: He gathers the lambs in His arms and carries them close to His heart; He gently leads those that have young."

"He tends His flock like a shepherd: He gathers the lambs in His arms and carries them close to His heart; He gently leads those that have young" Isaiah 40:11

The following is another way to look at being a barometer of your child – I call it "Root Parenting" and I describe it in the following blog post from my website.

Are you parenting the symptoms or reaching the roots?

VAL HARRISON, THE PRACTICALLY SPEAKING MOM·SUNDAY, AUGUST 19, 2018 Recently our family visited Mammoth Cave near Cave City, Kentucky. This is the largest known cave in the world with over 400 miles of mapped underground trails and caverns with another estimated 200 miles still to explore. Beneath the surface you can take all sorts of cave tours

- from "Domes and Dripstones" to the "Frozen Niagara."

Above the surface of this national park it seems like any other nature spot with creeks, walking trails and trees. You could be there, seeing all the above ground marvels and have no idea that you were only experiencing a small glimpse of the area's natural wonders when below the surface there may be running creek beds, tumbling rocks, and shifting layers. In fact, in 2014 a sudden giant sinkhole formed above Mammoth Cave that swallowed eight corvettes from the nearby National Corvette Museum. You see, what is below the surface can have a big impact on what happens above ground, whether you know what's going on down there or not.

Likewise, each of our kids have miles and miles of deeply forming questions, frustrations and fears. Their days are filled with just as much societal pressure, information overload, and internal conflict that we adults face daily. Unlike an adult, though, our children are trying to process and file all of these things in a brain that is still developing, and with a heart that is immature and easily swayed.

Our tendency as parents is to RESPOND to visible behaviors at face value rather than take the time to venture below the surface to the root cause. Reaching the roots is not an easy task for parents. I'm not here to guilt you or condemn; trust me when I say that I've missed the warning signs of an impending sinkhole more than once. After all, parents don't have the luxury of any road signs telling us "Speed bump" or "Curve ahead." No, the bigger the heart issue, the deeper it seems to reside and the more layers of surface area for us to peel away if we are to discover what's really happening with our kids.

Since I've had multiple children in all the growing stages, I've had plenty of opportunities to, regrettably, SURFACE PARENT. There have been peer wounds in elementary that I had no idea at the moment - like the time one of my sons was told by someone at a party, "you aren't into gaming and you're no good at sports so what's your life worth anyway?" There have been various lies from Satan (the enemy of our souls) that my children wrestled with. Such as the lie he told my daughter in the midst of great tragedy, "If God is good He wouldn't have allowed your friend's mom to die so either He isn't real, or He isn't good. Either way you might as well give up on Him because there's no point in following a god like that." And, regrettably, there have even been times when I have unknowingly caused deep emotional wounds in my child. Since I didn't know about the wound, I parented the rebellious behavior which only caused the wound to grow bigger and implant deeper underground. I can't tell you how devastating it is to discover such a deep chasm below the surface in your child's heart that you didn't know was there and, even worse, you didn't know you were the root cause. Parents, we don't get do overs. Each moment of parenting we are either Surface Parenting or Root Parenting.

Thankfully, God does redeem relationships!! He designed these amazing tools called *Apology, Restitution, Forgiveness, and Healing*. What a wonderful God we serve! But none of those can wipe away the past. Eventually, the scenarios that I mentioned earlier were revealed to me by my children so that I could walk with them through the process of belief correcting and heart mending. Root Parenting is far superior to Restoration Parenting, but both are necessary skills to hone.

Root Parenting requires extra time **observing** when we are busy with other things; it requires **listening with our heart** when we feel like snapping back; it means shouting a silent, pleading prayer for God to give us **discernment** when we feel like using our own judgement. Possibly hardest of all, it requires **slowing the pace of family life to make time for soul discussions and soul growth.** Parenting on the root level involves **wholehearted focus** on the souls of our kids and that is wildly difficult while completely essential.

You do realize that what I'm asking you to do is impossible - to accurately read the soul of another human, even if it is your own child? The only way you can discern the deeply complex tunnels buried below the surface of your child's behaviors is for you to be connected to the Creator of our souls, our all-knowing, all-loving Heavenly Father. Plant your roots deeply in His Word and regularly be nourished by Him. Only if you are committed to healthy roots in your own soul will you be able to identify the mysteries of your children's deep and complex root system.

Our pastor recently said, during a sermon on parenting, that every parent is going to mess up big with our kids. That was comforting to me as a parent with plenty of regrets. Mistakes are inevitable because we are imperfect humans, parenting immature imperfect humans.

Sometimes you're going to find yourself Surface Parenting instead of Root Parenting. Don't beat yourself up and stay that way. Instead *learn from your mistakes *ask your child for forgiveness *make sure YOUR roots are planted in the regular nourishment of the Word of God * and make a fresh commitment to keep digging deeper with this young person that He has entrusted to you. All the effort will result in an amazing tour of God's precious, hidden wonder - the soul of your child.

Prayerfully walking the parenting journey right along with you, Val

---

IF you would like to follow Val's blog, go to
www.PracticallySpeakingMOM.com

or find her on Facebook at

Val Harrison, The Practically Speaking MOM

And Instagram

Practically Speaking MOM

Part 2: Time-Saving Strategies for a Busy Family to Enjoy the Scenic View in the Fastlane of Life

This list, in part two of our book <u>Wearing All Your Hats Without Wearing Out</u>, is designed to help your family get into some habits that should free up your time to pursue the full, abundant life that God has planned for your family. My prayer is that this section would also help you to identify some potential pitfalls that your family may have fallen into. If you're busy spinning your wheels, arguing with your kids, or hearing them grumble through life, you're missing the blessings!

This is a family gathering at the Harrison house. We have seven kids; four are grown and are living on their own (two of whom are married) and we have two grand babies. Life has been busy for many years for this mama. **I understand overwhelmed, stressed, and tired, but it's such a great life!**

How can we possibly have time to enjoy life with our kids? Is it really possible to cherish the moments with our family, even in the fast lane of life?

I'd like to share some time management systems for the busy mama and her busy tribe.

1. **"No means no" and other ways words must mean what words mean; Getting Kids to Listen**

   (This first tip is a long one, but this is so important, so try to hang in there with me.)

   How much time does your family lose because your kids ignore what you say? You've tried so hard to patiently tell them multiple times, but they don't listen. You wind up being at your wits' end as so much time was consumed by a power-struggle over what should have been a simple, quick request.

   I'd like to show you an UNCOMPLICATED and EFFECTIVE WAY to increase your child's respect for your word. There's a change you can make that will decrease parental stress, as well as kid whining, manipulation, and begging; it can result in kids doing what they're told the first time.

Here it is: **Mean what you say or don't say it**.

In other words, YOU need to respect your word if you want your children to. Try to develop a personal parent motto of **"Say it ONCE, then ENFORCE."** If you tell a child, "stop it" or "let's go" or "pick up after yourself" (just some examples of things moms commonly say), if you tell them any of these things but then let them ignore you or delay,

 you're sending some very mixed messages which is creating some very unwanted habits in them as well as some negative beliefs about your words in their minds. You are making life more difficult for you and your kids by not clearly saying what you mean and then following up with it after the **first time** you say it. As the parent, you need to enforce what you've said **completely, consistently, and confidently**. If you're not willing to do that, then don't say it at all.

Step-by-Step Guide to Giving Your Voice Value to Your Kids:

*Slow down to give your words the attention they deserve. *Don't quickly rattle off a command.* Say it slow enough to really be heard, but first go through the following steps as well, before you make the command.

*Think before you speak and make sure you're willing to enforce your words after the first time you say it. *Think, "Is what I'm about to say consistent with what I want our standards to be in this family? Am I able to enforce this command right now?"*

*Make sure your child is really listening before you start talking. *Eye contact is a key in making sure they're listening. To get your child in the habit of giving you eye contact, you've got to be giving them eye contact too. Look at them, say their name and wait for them to look at you before you talk further. (Having them answer with a, "Yes, Mom?" Can also be helpful. You can do the same with them when they speak to you and it will help to turn this into the norm for communication at your house). Also, especially if they're young, get in closer proximity to your child, even*  *squatting down to be face-to-face. Taking the time to have eye contact and body proximity let's your child* *know that you think what you're about to say is important. It gives weight to words.*

Give clear instructions that are reasonable for your child's age and ability. If they are three or older, they may also be ready for some explanation about WHY you are making this command. You want your children to understand the principles behind your

rules so that they can begin to apply those same principles to future decisions and actions, then you want to start explaining the rule. For example, instead of saying, "get your shoes off the couch," you could say, "Tommy, I need you to get your shoes off of the couch. We don't put our shoes on the couch because we want the furniture to stay clean for us and any visitors, so Tommy, please get your shoes off the couch." (A word of caution here: My suggestion is that you tell them why BEFORE they ask you. If you give them an instruction and they respond with, "Why, Mommy?" that is setting in them a habit of thinking that they don't really need to obey until you give an adequate explanation for your request. That is NOT going to teach them to respect your word.

*Have them repeat back to you what you asked them to do, while you continue to make eye contact will insure that neither of you have an excuse to renege. *Let's say you want your child to take the clothes out*

of the dryer, put them in the laundry basket, and place the laundry basket on the couch. That's a lot of steps for a little guy to remember, or if this chore is new to him. He needs step-by- step, clear instructions and he needs to repeat these steps back to you so that you know for sure that he understands and will remember all those steps. If this is a task they've completed many times in the past, then step by step instructions may not be necessary, of course. It will be different for each child based on their age, ability, reliability, age, and previous experience.

*Hold to compliance to your word even when it is inconvenient for you to do so. *Did you just tell your daughter to go brush her teeth and she's sitting their looking at her book, not responding? Chances are that you didn't go over to her, get full eye contact, say her name before you said, "Emma, please go brush your teeth." Generally, they don't comply because you didn't give the instruction very well OR because they're in the habit of getting by without obeying. So, taking the time to do all of these steps will change that bad habit pretty quickly. If you will change your habits in how you GIVE instructions and being consistent in ENFORCING compliance, then you'll all be able to have more meaningful experiences for your family. You'll have more time to enjoy life in the fast lane!*

Here's an example of how future dialogues can sound at your house once you've brought more value to your words. It doesn't go this way every time at my house, but much of the time:

I might say, *"Emma,"* (then wait for her response).

"Yes, Mom."

"I'd like you to finish up that page of your book and then head upstairs and brush your teeth."

"Okay, Mom, I'll finish this page and then go brush my teeth."

'Thanks."

That's the dialog that can be in your family's future and it is wonderful because it eliminates a lot of nagging, complaining, ignoring, disobeying, frustration, and time-wasting! Yes, it takes time and effort to get these habits in place and you develop them step by step, not all at once. In the long run, it will be a much more pleasant life where you can actually focus on experiences rather than spending all of your time just trying to achieve compliance.

At our house, we also expect compliance in ATTITUDE along with ACTIONS as an equal value in following through. Learning that a negative attitude creates negative results, we just try to steer clear of whining, complaining, eye rolling, etc. Once a child gets out of these habits, you will see an improvement in relationships, in achievements, in experiences, in enjoyment and peace, and an improvement in how much time it takes to complete a task.

All of these actions are what makes up the parental life skill of <u>Making Your Voice Matter</u>. "Say it ONCE, then ENFORCE" will save your family loads of time in the long run, once you've given your kids a chance to see that "a new mom is in town and this one means what she says." If you want your kids to experience a blessed and successful life, at some point they've got to learn to honor the person in authority, whether it's a boss, a teacher, a police officer, or YOU. The younger you help them develop this into a success habit, the quicker they'll start reaping the rewards that are available to them from all kinds of life situations.

Not only that, but the younger you begin, the easier it is to implement. When a child starts crawling is a good time to begin "Say it ONCE, then ENFORCE" as a parent. My grown daughter has done a great job of this with her little guys. Our twenty-two-month-old grandson, James, already enjoys the peace and blessings that come from honoring his mom and dad's "no" or "wait" or "say 'please' first."

GRANDSONS JAMES AND ASHER WITH THEIR MOM, BECCA, ON THE LEFT, AND ANOTHER OF OUR DAUGHTERS, ABBY.

It is such a blessing to a Grandparent (or anyone else who may be put in charge of your child) to babysit a little guy that is in the habit of obeying. Let's take my grandson Jamey as an example, when he's told, "Jamey, don't touch that, it might break" or "Jamey, don't go into that room, someone is sleeping in there," James is obedient about these commands because his parents have consistently followed through with their word after the first time he's told something.

I remember once I was babysitting Jamey at about 16 months old. While I was holding his new baby brother Asher, across the room Jamey started to pick up an extension cord that was plugged in. I said, "No, Jamey, ow." I watched his little face immediately crumple up when he heard me say, "no" because he knew that "no" means "no." I could tell his mind was wrestling with his desires. He started to fuss a little, but then whispered to himself, "no, no, no." Then he took a step back from the chord and looked for something else to play with. This was a quick self-correction with very little negative emotions. It was the sweetest thing ever to observe a little toddler who had learned self-control. That doesn't happen easily; it is the result of parents giving consistent effort to make their words matter. Be a parent who makes your words matter. You will find that it will benefit you, your children, and your family, along with blessing everyone they are with!

If you verbally make family rules and then you don't enforce them, you're simply teaching your kids to disregard your word, and, honestly, it affects how much respect they have for you. It is hard to respect someone whose words are worthless even to the one saying them. So, be more careful, parents, to only say

it if you mean it. If you say it, then follow through with it after you say it the first time.

As parents, it's great to say "yes" as much as you can, but when you must say, "no," "No" must mean "no." Otherwise your No means, *"beg more and mom might let you."* Or when you ask them to do something, but you don't follow-up on whether they obey, you're teaching your kids that *"If I ignore what Mom told me to do, then I probably won't end up having to do it."*

Save your family plenty of arguing, nagging, confusion, and frustration by being CLEAR with what you say, and then CONSISTENTLY enforce COMPLETE follow-through. The level of peace will increase in your home by leaps and bounds! Yay for Consistent Parents!

2. Perfection is the Worst!

For the second practical tip in saving time in a busy household, you want to see that PERFECTION is not what you should be pursuing for your family. It's so time-consuming and emotionally draining to have a standard of perfection for yourself, your kids, or your family. Since perfection isn't possible, you essentially set yourself up for feeling like a failure at a non-attainable standard. Especially if the task you're working on is not connected to a relationship, then it really doesn't deserve so much pressure. Yes, we should do quality work and represent ourselves, our family, and our God well as we put our signature on anything we do, but at the end of our lives, what matters most are the memories we've made and the relationships we've given time to; so, please, please, don't waste time and emotional stress on being a failing perfectionist!   <u>Do your BEST within BALANCE and learn to be CONTENT with that.</u>

This is a great example to set for your kids as well. If you are raising a little detailed person, he can easily set his expectations at "perfect" and find himself constantly struggling to

1- START the project because he's afraid he won't do it perfectly

2- FINISH a task because it's not yet perfect

3- FEEL CONTENT with what he accomplished because it could still be better

If you have a young perfectionist at your house, they're probably also the one who takes forever to get something done. Model a better perspective for them.

Here are a few of the common phrases you'll hear me saying to my kids:

* "Do your BEST with BALANCE and learn to be CONTENT with that"

* "If you've done your best and LEARNED from your mistakes, then that is success!"

*"Do things with excellence, but not perfection."

Can you tell that I speak from experience? Not only in my own life, but my husband and two sons and one daughter are all perfectionists by nature. Yikes! That's a lot of stress, frustration, and unhappiness, because perfection is an unattainable standard. If perfection is the standard, then it's stressful *while you're working*, disappointing and frustrating *when*

*Success is...
giving your best
effort and
learning from
your mistakes.*

OUR YOUNGEST SON,
ANDREW

you're finished, and unmotivating for *future endeavors* because you've experienced constantly falling short of the standard. A better standard is EXCELLENCE or GIVING MY BEST EFFORT AND LEARNING FROM THE MISTAKES ALONG THE WAY. Pursue one of those standards instead of perfection.

3. "Teamwork makes the dream work." It's a popular saying for a reason.

Our third tip for saving time in your family is to value Teamwork.

Teamwork is good for a family because

*it makes your busy family life more doable when everyone chips in and helps

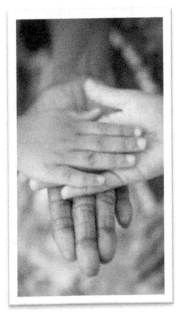

*work is GOOD FOR KIDS

*working TOGETHER is bonding for a family.

From everyone cleaning up the kitchen after dinner, to remodeling a room, to working on the yard, hard work is good for the soul and doing it together is good for the soul of the family.

Just yesterday my husband, Rich, asked our daughter Abby what some of her favorite family memories were. The one she mentioned first was when it was "hay baling season." All the kids would jump on the back of the truck and ride through the field back to the newly-baled hay. Once there, some of them would jump off to throw the bales up to the truck while the others would stack them. Then they'd unload them all into the barn. It was really hard work. It didn't always feel fun at the time, yet as the kids look back on it they remember it fondly and are thankful for the memories. **Hard work together as a family is a great blessing.**

This is one of my favorite pictures of a family work day from the past. My husband had told the boys to help him chop some wood, clean up the woodpile, and get a bonfire prepped. My son Nathan (the lumber jack in the picture) was always finding funny personalities to be when he was young. You never knew if he was going to spend a month talking with an Australian accent, being an old man walking with a cane, or trying to be the cook from the Muppets, but one thing was for sure -- he'd always find a *fun* way to do life, even work. While he had outgrown these clever interpretations, for the most part, on this day he gave us a little nod to his earlier years. In the background is our son, Josh, who is our dry-humored practical jokester. Clearly, he's trying to illustrate that this is very hard work and that throwing your head back and closing your eyes is a great way to saw a log. (Don't try this at home, it's not a good idea. But don't worry, he wasn't really sawing at that moment, he just wanted to make a fun memory for the camera).

My guess is that if you're reading this book, you're feeling stressed or burned out in your role as mother. Is it possible that some of the tasks that you have taken on personally are projects that could be tackled as a family or a small group within the family? Along with developing many important character qualities, hard work as a team can be great bonding for a family. **Give your kids the gift of teamwork and get in there and get things done *together*!**

4. RE-EVALUATE how you spend your EMPLOYMENT.

It's so easy to feel the pressure of time without really evaluating how we're using our time. I'm guilty of that as well. Are we using it on what we really care about most or have we just kind of gotten into a groove and are mindlessly "stuck" in it? With our mouth we say, "I'm too busy, I need a break" all while we are working more and more hours at a job to pay for nice cars, big TVs and the cable bills that go with them, the latest iPhones, and eating out. If you or your spouse has the option to cut some employment hours by cutting out some big-ticket items, then do so! The time you would've spent working to pay for those

luxuries, replace that with family time that is free but truly rewarding such as **volunteering as a family** (we go to a nursing home once a month to play games with the residents and just visit with them, for example), or invite someone over for a meal (an activity that has become almost obsolete), and you'll find yourselves blessed as well.

While we're on this topic, I just have to mention that if you're not currently a stay-at-home mom, but you'd like to be, it is more doable than you might think. You may need to gradually head home (working part time for a while before quitting all together). Another option is working from home. That's one of the reasons I have sold Mary Kay for almost twenty years and now my daughter, Becca, does also, so that she can stay home with her boys. Any number of hours that you can reduce at your job to have more time with your kids will pay off in far more valuable ways than money. God will bless the sacrifice you make to set aside greater income for greater family time.

5. Save your Sanity with a MEAL PREP PLAN.

If you have heard of freezer cooking but don't have time, I've got a one-hour-per-week plan for you! **Visit my website and blog,**

www.PracticallySpeakingMOM.com **for lots of time-saving organization tips. Or go directly to my Sanity Meal Prep blog post: http://practicallyspeakingmom.com/homeorganiz ation/meal-** freezer-plan/ for meal prep that can make it more possible for kids to help AND will also save you lots of time in the kitchen!

6. Papers To-Go

Oh my goodness, we moms have SO MANY PAPERS we have to deal with every day! It is time to take control of your mail and all the papers that come as a constant stream into your house. Here's my motto for helping with this issue: **"ONE and DONE"**

As I mentioned earlier, for about twenty years I've been a <u>Mary Kay</u> <u>consultant</u>. For several of those years I was a director who drove a free car. I earned four free cars to be exact and did this all while homeschooling my children. I don't tell you that to brag, but just to let you know that that kind of accomplishment is doable only with some serious time management. I learned a lot of great time control strategies during my years in Mary Kay training, including a paper plan called, "One and Done."

"ONE and DONE" means touch a paper once and deal with it right then. The way I implement that at my house includes my mail basket. All mail and papers should go directly into your mail basket first. Resist the urge to thumb through all those papers unless you really have time to deal with them. Once a day or every couple of days, grab your mail basket along with the following items:

A.   File Folders that are labeled "Bills" "Events" "Important Documents to Process" "Coupons" "Things of Interest"

A. Family Calendar
B. Bill Calendar
C. To-Do Notebook

As you pick up each item out of the basket, determine right then how to "pile" it. It will either go in the Recycle pile (or trash), in the Bills pile, Events pile, Important Documents pile, Coupons pile, or in the Things of Interest pile.

Once you've sorted all the papers into those six piles, you're ready to deal them!

*Take the Events pile and add each event to your Family Calendar. If you want to keep the paper as an information reference, then place it in the Events Folder.

*Enter all of the bills into the Bill Calendar and then place them in the Bills folder until they've been paid.

*Add the important documents to process to my To-Do List followed by placing them in their folder OR process them right then.

In my <u>To-Do List notebook</u>, I start a new page each day and move the items forward from the day before that didn't get done the previous day. I have a similar one that is my <u>CHORES Notebook</u>. Let's say I'm walking through the kitchen, see the microwave and say to myself, *"Oh my, there are so many fingerprints on the front of the microwave that it looks like an octopus was playing tic tac toe!"* Well, I simply write "front of microwave" in the CHORES notebook. Then each day when I make the kids' chores, I add those items to the list or add it to my own chore list for me, or I use the list as a handy way to give extra chores to a child who's needing an extra chore for their character development.

Reasons Why I Might Give an Extra Chore generally have to do with displaying a rottin ATTITUDE or ACTION when given a task:

*POOR ATTITUDE - If a bad attitude is being displayed when I ask them to do something, I'm going to give them additional work to do because they clearly haven't worked enough to learn to realize that hard work won't hurt them and can bring a lot of rewards, such as self-satisfaction for a job well done, physical activity that increases endorphins, and the contentment that comes from knowing they're contributing to the good of the team.

A couple days ago I told my youngest, "Honey, I'm going to need to continue to give you extra dishes to wash until your attitude about washing dishes changes." Boy, did that create a sudden turn-around in the little one's disposition. I was able to follow, shortly with, "that is a great improvement in your attitude. You'll enjoy your day a lot more with a good attitude and so will everyone around you. You're finished! Go and enjoy your free time!"

*POOR ACTIONS - Maybe they didn't complete a chore. Let's say they vacuumed but failed to put the vacuum away. Or maybe they were refilling the soap dispenser but left a big mess of

soap on the outside of the dispenser. Or perhaps they failed to have some good living habit, like not cleaning up after themselves when they made a sandwich. <u>Any of these actions will continue to happen again and again in the future if the child never receives an unpleasant outcome from their irresponsible action.</u> So, now it's time for you, the parent, to figure out what to do about their offense. You're trying to figure out what consequence might be appropriate for the failure to perform to the standard you've set for their capability. But first, stop, Parent!

Before you give them an added chore for their poor-quality work, ask yourself:

> A. *"Have I made the standard clear to them in the past?"*
> B. *"Is the standard something they are capable of fulfilling?"*
> C. *"Have I eve shown them what good quality work looks like on this task – do they know HOW to achieve the standard?"*

If you haven't, then you need to go find them and show them how to do it right. Then watch them redo it as well. Now you've done your part to train them to a quality standard.

Do your part before you expect them to do their part.

7. The DIN DIN Club

There was a silly jingle we used to say as Mary Kay directors, *"I'm a member of the DIN DIN Club, **Do it now, Do it now, Do it now.**"* That might be silly to say, but there's nothing silly about the huge amount of time you can gain just by developing this mindset with tasks.

Today my eight-year-old forgot to put her dish in the dishwasher after eating, so I told her that I wanted her to do that plus as a way to help her remember next time, I asked her to also wash the table (that's kind of my thing – if you leave things out, I'm going to give you a job related to those things. This really helps everyone to better pick up after themselves at our house). Anyway, I asked her to do that and then I walked off to do some other things myself. When I returned to check on her progress (because I want my word to be valued, so I need to follow-up on how well she followed through) she was standing in the same spot as when I left, waiting to ask me if she needed to wash the table with a soapy wash cloth or just brush the crumbs into the trash. Now, it is true that I could have and should have asked her if she had any questions before I left the room, but the truth is, she could have already been finished washing it with soap and water by the time I came back into the room. What a time waster it was to stand around waiting to see if she could do the "easier" version of the job. Let's be people who have a motto of "do it now" instead of a habit of procrastination that says, "how little can I do?" and "how long can I hold off doing it?" That lousy habit will keep your to-do list very long and you'll accomplish so much less than just rolling up your sleeves and diving in to the work with all of your might, right now. **Do it now! Do it now!**

7. "Keep it Real" for Real

Are you familiar with the story of the Trojan Horse (a gift that appeared to be very generous but actually contained a hidden danger that destroyed a gated and well-protected city)? Most homes in America today contain just as dangerous a "treasure" and we love it so much that most of us couldn't imagine life without it. It's our TV's, internet, and game systems. My home is no different on this issue -- we love our shows and our Google and our social media, but within lurks an ugly monster masquerading as innocent entertainment. The filth, timewasting factor, and addiction to the screen all seem to increase at an alarming rate in American homes. I find myself, as a parent who desperately cares for my children's souls and minds, more and more concerned, saddened, and angry with the war that has been waged against our souls right in our own homes. In addition to the mental and moral

harm that can come from an unbridled internet, it also seems
to produce apathy about life in general. Americans today are easily bored and impatient with anything that's not highly entertaining, but we're also highly UN-motivated to advance and accomplish. As family interaction is at an all- time low in our society, sadly, many live daily enthralled in watching reality TV while not creating their own real-life MEANINGFUL reality. TV and social media are robbers of our time and destroyers of our soul, so guard against these in yourself and be continually watching for signs of excess in your kids as well.

Recently on the Glen Beck radio show he cited a study that said that teenagers average nine hours a day on social media. Nine hours! You want to talk about a time waster, boy that's our biggest culprit!

(In our home we also have many safeguards regarding the filth that abounds online that, even innocently and unintentionally our children can stumble across. That is a topic for another day. Currently I'm working on a blog post for my website called, "The Filtering MOM" so if you have filters, movie review cites, or media policies at your house that you'd like to share with me, I'd love to hear from you to add to my list for people to reference. Our family also has an internet agreement that we have our kids sign and we ask them accountability questions based on that agreement. Likewise, my husband and I also hold each other accountable and we let our kids know that.

We need to model for our kids what responsible, self-controlled adulthood looks like if we want them to become responsible, self-controlled adults.

9. Cut it out!

Do you feel like you spend half of your time trying to sort out and deal with all the little things that kids can accumulate! Sometimes I feel like my home is a giant puzzle board with all these little pieces to find their spot to put it all together, but more pieces keep appearing. For example, with four daughters total, I've had at least one little girl in my house constantly for the past 24 years and in those years I'm pretty sure that I've picked up a minimum of five hundred pony tails throughout our house in all kinds of odd places every.single.day.for.years. Ahhh,

the puzzle pieces of life that makes me crazy!

Our middle two girls, Abby and Becca.

Our oldest and youngest daughters, Tori and Emma

I've finally realized, after all this time, that if a girl only owned a few pony tails, she'd be more careful with them. Thus, my eighth tip for you - get rid of all the excess. **Cut out the excess to reduce the**

stress! Really, bundle it up and get it out! If you find that you're spending a lot of time LOOKING for something at home, it either indicates that you need to improve your family's HABIT of everything having a place and putting it there every time, OR you've simply got too much stuff! What hoard have you started that needs to be eliminated to cut out the time it takes to deal with the stuff?

For me, my hoarding is of homeschool curriculum. Oh, how I love books, especially educational books! But my kids are mostly grown, and I have too much. So, I sorted and kept what I love that can't be replaced easily and sold the rest on some

 Facebook groups I'm in. I made about $300 last weekend selling curriculum to people who picked it up off my front porch. Kudos to Facebook selling!

10. Plan, then Play! It's the best way! Let me just confess to you right now that I and my husband are pretty boring people. We have a hard time relaxing and having fun. We are much more task-oriented than people-oriented and that has been a real on-going problem throughout our years of parenting.

A FEW SILLY ANTICS WHILE VISITING A PEACH FARM

Gradually, we have learned the sacred value of play, laughter, fun, and memory-making. Something God has been re-focusing with me, yet again, is the importance of these relationship moments. We've always been very future-minded and have been laser-focused on helping our children to be well-prepared for life. While we strive for making the future better, hustling hard each day for a bright future for our kids, we may be missing out on the best days of our lives.

I don't want to waste the best days. Yes, we need to plan, we need to do our work with excellence, and we need to have systems that we enforce with clear and confident consistency, but we also need to play! Celebrate! Make memories! These moments are quickly fleeting. Don't forget to <u>enjoy the ride</u> in the fast lane – take the scenic route!

Here's a list of a few ways I've learned to savor the scenic view while we're running in the fast lane:

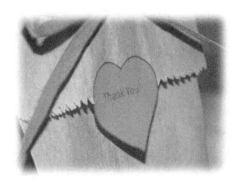

*Making homemade cards and homemade treats with my youngest two daughters

*Taking unexpected detours with the kids to the local gelato shop or Snow Cone Hut to give the kids a cold treat

OUR SON-IN-LAW DAKOTA WITH OUR GRANDSON JAMEY

91

*Going to a nursery and letting the kids pick out some flowers to plant in the garden and getting one for their bedroom too

*Leaving little notes on their bedroom door (just one more great use for sticky notes - one of my all-time favorite things!)

*Listening to adventure books on CD when the family is in the car (our favorites are Adventures in Odyssey, Jonathan Parks, Focus on the Family Radio Theatre, Lamplighter books).

JonathanPark.com

Lamplighter.net

Whitsend.org

Focusonthefamily.com/radio-theatre

*Playing lots of games as a family. Our favorites are Monopoly Deal, Ticket to Ride (play as partners), Telestrations, Dutch Blitz, Pandemic

*Volunteer at a nursing home together. Once a month we go to a nursing home. Our kids perform some music (which motivates the residents to come out of their rooms) and then we play games with them. This has been rewarding in so many ways for our family. It has taught our kids better  communication skills, given them compassion for those who are lonely (so many of them have no one at all who comes to visit them) and it's been a great bonding time for us as well.

I'd love to hear what your family does to enjoy the Scenic Route while you run in the Fast Lane of Life! You can visit my website at www.PracticallySpeakingMOM.com and share your ideas for family relationship building.
Appendix, Parenting Resource:

MERCY SEAT PARENTING:

A Merciful Attitude as You, Unwaveringly Direct Your Child's Character Toward God's Standard

In an earlier season in my parenting, as I studied scripture to see how God, our Heavenly Father, parented, Exodus 25: 17-22 was a passage that stuck out to me. This is from the Old Testament, when God is instructing His people about how to build the Tabernacle where He would reside. He was going to dwell in the Ark of the Covenant which was placed in the most sacred of all of the areas in the Tabernacle. This room was called the Holy of Holies. On top of the Ark of the Covenant, God had them fashion out of gold something He called the

> *Mercy Seat Parenting is an empathetic and patient approach of heading toward God's ideals for our lives, for our good and His glory while remaining firm on the standards and boundaries.*

Mercy Seat. What do you think of when you hear those words? I think of sitting together with our Heavenly Father and experiencing mercy from Him. That is the feeling He must have wanted to convey, or He wouldn't have called it the Mercy Seat. Then if you read on, He describes what the Mercy Seat was for. He said, this is the place where He would "discuss his decrees and laws." What? Wait a minute. "Discuss his decrees and laws?" that doesn't sound all kind and merciful. That sounds unbending, maybe rigid. So why would he name it the Mercy Seat? I believe He gave it that name because He wanted us to know that while His standards don't change, He is merciful and approachable. He wants us to come to Him and feel safe with Him. A good judge is one who listens intently, seeks all the pertinent information, is wise and measured in His response. He is fair. Our

Heavenly Father wanted us to know that He is fair and approachable even though His standards do no change. The Mercy Seat was His special place for us to truly experience His great love and wisdom even though His standards are unchanging and fixed.

We can parent like this as well with an attitude of, "Son, this is the standard for how we are going to treat people. Now we need to help you move toward the standard. I don't expect you to be perfect, but I expect you to be making improvements in your attitudes, actions, and words that align with God's standards for our lives."

"THE MERCY SEAT" WAS A LABEL GOD GAVE TO THE VERY CENTRAL TOP OF THE ARK OF THE COVENANTENT, WHERE GOD WOULD MEET WITH THE HIGH PRIESTS TO "DISCUSS HIS LAWS AND DECREES." GOD USED THE WORDS "MERCY SEAT" BECAUSE HE WANTED IT TO REPRESENT HIMSELF AS APPROACHABLE, HAVING GRACE IN THE MIDST OF HIS UNWAVERING STANDARDS FOR LIVING."

Val Harrison, The Practically Speaking MOM

Meet the Practically Speaking MOM

Val is blessed to be wife of Rich for 26 years, mom to seven children (including two married daughters and their husbands), homeschool mom for 20 years, Grandma to two perfect grandsons, speaker, author, and a speech teacher at homeschool co-ops.

"While my greatest desire is to serve my Lord Jesus, I am thankful that He has given me a passion for helping parents in their great responsibility of developing a strong family. I share the messages God has given me to encourage and equip parents to recognize that their family is God's masterpiece.

I enjoy speaking at women's groups, parenting conferences, and homeschool conventions where I seek to share practical advice through a "tell it like it is" style of a little humor and wisdom – wisdom that I've only gained through all the many mom-fails and follies. Thankfully, God's grace fills in the gaps where our abilities fall short!

With a degree in Speech Communications, I have enjoyed teaching Speech classes for the past 19 years to help students develop their speaking skills for both public and interpersonal settings (such as job interviews and conflict resolution) through fun and practical exercises. I thrive on motivating students to communicate effectively, sincerely, and for God's glory!"

My prayer is that the words of my mouth and the thoughts of my heart would be pleasing in His sight for He is my Rock and my Redeemer!
(Psalm 19:14)"

Here's a few of my blog posts from PracticallySpeakingMOM.com

"What to do with the Sad Little Sisters: Seasons of Change"

"Save Your Sanity: The One-Hour-a Week Quick Freezer Plan"

When Littles are Loud; Maximizing the Moments without Drowning in Chaos

(This is a blog series, e-book, and book)

"This Moment is Your Legacy"

"More than a Lemonade Stand: Preparing Your Student for the Pursuit of a Career "

"A List of Resources to Help Kids Get God's Word and Wisdom into Their Hearts"

Practical Tips for Christian Parents
Raising Teenagers:
3 Ways to Improve the
Parent/Teen Relationship

WWW.PRACTICALLYSPEAKINGMOM.COM

100

More books by the Practically Speaking MOM:

From the Series "Our Family God's Masterpiece"

Clash in Your HOME

A GAME PLAN FOR CLEANING UP THE CONFLICT

KAL HARRISON
THE PRACTICALLY SPEAKING MOM

Made in the USA
Middletown, DE
06 December 2018